Soft Zipper

SOFT ZIPPER

OBJECTS • FOOD • ROOMS

George Bowering

Introduction by Lisa Robertson

VANCOUVER
NEW STAR BOOKS
2021

◯ NEW STAR BOOKS LTD

#107–3477 Commercial St, Vancouver, BC V5N 4E8 CANADA

1574 Gulf Road, #1517 Point Roberts, WA 98281 USA

newstarbooks.com · info@newstarbooks.com

The publisher acknowledges the financial support of the Canada Council for the Arts, the British Columbia Arts Council, and the Government of Canada.

Cataloguing information for this book is available from Library and Archives Canada, www.collectionscanada.gc.ca.

Cover design by Oliver McPartlin

Typeset by New Star Books

Printed and bound in Canada by Imprimerie Gauvin, Gatineau, QC

First printing March 2021

INTRODUCTION

BUTTON KOSMOS

LISA ROBERTSON

George Bowering is writing *Soft Zipper* in Jalisco in a rented holiday apartment. He's writing in the Vancouver condominium he shares with his wife Jean, in his triangular study. And he's writing within and with the memory of other rooms, other spaces — the porch of his old rambling house in Kerrisdale, the artist Greg Curnoe's Richmond Street studio in London Ontario, his mother's kitchen table in Oliver B.C., his cherished ballpark, the Roman room John Keats died in. "Prose is a spatial experience" George said in a 1979 interview, and it's clear in these pages that memory is too. The supple scale of space, from dresser drawer to American road trip, here folds and regroups the poet's craft — for George's prose is poet's prose, with its joyous attention to the detail of syntax, the humour and mystery of juxtaposition, and the music of tone.

Soft Zipper, a fragmented anti-memoir which organizes a lifetime of vignettes and recollections around a resolutely objective, rather than subjective point of view, borrows a structure, and subtitles — Objects, Food, Rooms — from American modernist Gertrude Stein's 1914 volume *Tender Buttons*. What Stein discovered in writing her prose poems (also while on holiday, but in Spain), was that space is a synthetic perception. We compose it retrospectively with glimpses, borrowings, visual and musical rhymes and puns, and the staccato movement of our attention. In *Tender Buttons* the domestic detritus assembled by early Cubists in their still life collages finds its way across into her prose poems, and becomes there a plastic field of syntactic experiment, "the rhythm of the visible world" as she later explained. Where Stein's ear is playfully abstract, or at least abstracting, George's sound sense is vernacular, keyed to the plain pleasures of familiar speech. William Carlos Williams, rather than Eric Satie, would be a sonic predecessor. Prose is a domestic production here. His spaces too are often fabricated and fleshed out in accordance with the homely pleasure of touch. The feel of his father's homemade felt skullcap in his hands is the first haptic foray, and soon after those same hands — in sweet homage to Stein — are plunged into a big glass bowl of buttons at his grandmother's house. The writers' hands remain present throughout this book, holding combs, baseballs, the remote control, reminding us also that this prose is *made,* and by hand too, at a table. It is a writing table, a long table, a deal table, an outdoor table, a kitchen table where cribbage or canasta is played, his old professor Warren Tallman's mahogany table, and it is a rhythmic point of return: hands do something at a table repeatedly, usually with others. "How did he make it work" George asks of his father and his little skullcap. It is one of the questions we might bring as readers into his book.

Our company in these pages is excellent. Charles Olson, Ornette Coleman, Samuel Beckett, Roland Barthes, George Oppen, Greg Curnoe: George slips his literary and artistic heroes and mentors into his texts casually, almost on the sly, much in the way that, as a professor, he'd carry extra books to the seminar table, fetish authors not on the syllabus. He'd teach the class without mentioning or presenting them to us, simply placing them a little rakishly in front of him, mysterious accessories to the topic at hand. We could read the spines if we stretched our necks. We learned to jot down those titles in our notebooks and follow up in the library. In this way we were tempted towards the books of Kristeva, Wittgenstein, Cixous. George's oblique address wittily complicates *Soft Zipper* too. But here the prose itself, and its relationship to personal memory, relates less to the punned-upon *Tender Buttons* and its synthetic cubism than it does to the vocal patterns of *The Autobiography of Alice B. Toklas*, Stein's 1932 memoir, with its soft hint of pastiche of a recently past era of domestic English. Stein played on her partner

Alice Toklas's voice with its wryly obsessive precision regarding the sensuality of household economics; in George's book the homely diction delights in a word like "snazzy", but it can also swerve meta-textually to Olson's theoretical propositions on the body as object among objects. In *Soft Zipper* I'd say the voice is not far from his old seminar cadences — a light, cajoling, self-ironical performance of George Bowering the nationally lauded writer, George Bowering the voracious and careful and ever-curious reader, by George Bowering the scallywag boy from Oliver.

I first studied Stein in George's classroom at Simon Fraser University in 1986. Rereading now, I'm in the yellowing pages of the Van Vechten *Selected* with the Picasso portrait of Stein on the cover, which we used in his class. I kept the copy that George assigned as a course text for his undergrad seminar on modernist prose; my faint pencil underlining and occasional class notes are there on the brittle paper, joined now by several more decades of marginal reading marks. I recall reading Hemingway too for that class, and

Ondaatje's *Coming Through Slaughter*, always ignited by George's infectiously enthusiastic curiosity — how does it work? How does the sentence work? What is the syntax doing? And again I am guided, as George has been too, by Stein, this time her essay "Composition as Explanation", also on our syllabus back in 1986.

In this lecture, written in 1925 at the car garage as she watched mechanics work on her old Ford, Stein makes three timely and still exciting discoveries about the composition of prose. Each is inherent to the texts in *Soft Zipper* — George has carried them into the time of his own composing. One is *the continuous present*, the next is *beginning again*, and the third is *using everything*. By means of these three techniques, which are deeply those of the bricoleur, the home mechanic, the homemaker, the writer stays within the consciousness of the manual and cognitive activity of writing in real time. This is a conduct. In 1986 or 2006 or last week I underlined Stein's words in pencil:

Each period of living differs from any other period of living not in the way life is but in the way life is conducted and that authentically speaking is composition. After life has been conducted in a certain way everybody knows it but nobody knows it, little by little, nobody knows it as long as nobody knows it. Any one creating the composition in the arts does not know it either, they are conducting life and that makes their composition what it is, it makes their work compose as it does.

The writer makes sentences that express the ongoing re-composition of language in relation to memory and experience. Memory and experience are in the present only: they too are compositions, moving syntheses of seized-upon fragments. And so their interleaving by means of the sentence creates that little bit of freshness or strangeness that lifts what can be said. Life, composition, text: a conduct.

George said in an interview in 2007 "the sentence is what you want, the sentence that is very clear but mysterious at the same time." This mystery is the kind that's routinely observed at the writing table. It's the abidingly common mystery of how we conduct ourselves — in the sentence, in the kitchen, in love — that reveals itself in the syntax only. We might consider conduct as another word for cosmology, where both of these are lodged firmly in the chaotic delight of everyday life, where the bashed-up tuba's wounds add to the higher notes. Parts are observable, and parts occur on the sly. Order is made by combining the visible and invisible. Prose does present a cosmos, as does the baseball diamond or the radio or the skullcap decorated with astrology cut-outs or the mimeographed poetry zine — I think here of George's old magazine Beaver Kosmos. Now you're holding one of the commonplace mysteries of the composition of time in your hands.

SOFT ZIPPER

OBJECTS

In this (after all) conventional debate
between science and subjectivity, I had
arrived at this curious notion: why mightn't
there be, somehow, a new science for each
object? A *mathesis singularis* (and no longer
universalis)?

                 – Roland Barthes, *Camera Lucida*

THE SKULLCAP

In the bottom of a drawer beside the bed in our condominium there is a piece of dusty old felt. Once in a while I give it a feel with my crooked fingers and I get a rush of dirty sweet feeling for my childhood curiosity. The thing is a folded skullcap with little shapes cut out of the felt — stars, half-moons, planets, triangles. Every morning of my childhood and whenever I was home after that, I would see this soft blue half-ball on my father's head, where it had the job of smoothing his tangled brown hair. One time I asked about this cap and he told me he had made it when he was a schoolboy, and so I knew why it was as small on his dome as a yarmulke, though of course I didn't know what that was. Now here I am, a man quite a bit older than he ever got, and all these decades later I wonder about two things concerning my father the skullcap maker. How did he and his classmates, if he did this work in a class at school or at his church camp, make these

5

perfect little astrology holes in the felt, and more important, how did he make it work as a cap on his head? Not a flat circle but half of a hollow ball? Over the years after I somehow acquired or inherited it — I must have told my mother and brothers it was the only thing I wanted — I would try it on, but though I habitually wear hats of one sort or the other, I have never worn this skullcap out of the house, and never for longer than a minute inside the house. Yet I have kept it since my father died half a century ago. I saw it just this morning, while I sat on the edge of the bed, my hair in an awful tangle.

THE GUN

    When I was in grade three I felt unarmed. All the boys had guns, or wished they had guns. I wished that I had a gun. The most popular game for boys was guns. Some of the time we played swords, so we all had skinned knuckles that made our mothers look up at the ceiling. A few years later, after my family moved into town, I had a famous sword that had been through innumerable battles. It had serious dents, but a lot of enemy swordsmen had lost their wooden blades in unfortunate challenges. But back when I was in grade three my parents somehow got wind of the fact that I pined for a gun. As far as I knew, the only way a boy could get a gun was in the form of a Christmas or birthday present. In the weeks previous to my eighth birthday I must have been ramping up the hints, walking around the house or outside, manouevering between apple trees, pointing at invisible adversaries with a crooked twig, and making that boy's expulsive mouth sound that does not in the least resemble the report of a real revolver or automatic. On the first day of December, my birthday, in case you wanted to know, arrived, and yes, Georgie got his gun. I immediately performed my fictional thanks. Guns were supposed to be constructed of some metal, and came, if they were revolvers, in a belted holster, and if they were automatics they should have looked like the kind of steel that kidnappers and Nazis were afraid of. My gun was made of rather softish wood, a kind of squarish thing. When I pulled the trigger (you could not squeeze that item that was probably kept taut by a rubber band), it said click.

THE CHERRY LADDER

I was lucky. About the time I was old enough to work in the orchards, the aluminum ladders were replacing the heavier wooden ones. Before I got out of the fruit-picking profession, the Giraffes and little Gyrettes had appeared, to speed up the process or cut the orchardist's labour expenses. These were the high-bucket machines that people now call cherry-pickers. People now say cherry-pick when they mean taking the individual item you fancy rather than gathering the whole shebang. That's exactly the opposite of the way you pick cherries. Here is another way they have made the work quicker and less expensive for the orchardists: instead of nice big trees in rows with space to set a ladder, they crop short little semi-espaliered trees, so you can practically harvest your peaches or apples while standing on the ground. Or else they have yanked out all the fruit trees and replaced them with rows and rows of grape vines. Back in the time of real trees, apple-picking season would coincide with the first weeks of the school year. We boys would be told that if our grades were looking as if they would be good, we'd be let out of school to head for the orchards to make money. But I think we knew that fruit was relentless in its ripening, and the orchardists would be eager to find someone to get up those ladders. My father the school teacher spent the daylight hours of the summer in someone's orchard. I could never keep up with him, but he gave me lots of advice so that I could try. The one I like best was that the safest rung to stand on is the top one, and he was right. When you are picking cherries, that is the top of a 24-foot ladder, and you have a long wire hook to pull down the supple cherry-loaded branches higher than that.

TWO BOWLS

I loved going to visit or stay with my grandfather and grandmother. They lived almost forty miles up the valley, and when I was really little, my grandfather was the postmaster up there. My grandmother was a good old-fashioned Baptist grandmother who was once named Clara Miller, can you imagine? I called him Grandpa and her Grandma. My mother's father and stepmother we didn't see so often. I called him Granddad and I don't remember calling her anything. When I was a boy, say nine or eleven, pretty soon after arriving at their house behind the post office I would be into Grandma's two big glass bowls, the button bowl and the picture bowl. The latter was filled with black and white photographs of everyone in the family from years ago right up to the present. I spent hours looking through those pictures, no matter how many times I had seen them. There was a picture of my grandparents with all their offspring, Llew, Grace, my father

Ewart, Ella, Jack, Gerry, and Dorothy, who had died when I was a toddler. In this family picture my father had a bald head. Grandma told me, with simulated impatience, that as soon as he heard there was going to be a family picture, he went and shaved his head. I loved this because it was so unlike my dad, except that it was secretly just like him. I knew that my Baptist grandmother sort of liked it inside, and I wanted to be just like my dad. The other bowl was just as big and contained hundreds and hundreds of buttons. I thought I must have a really big family that had been here for a long time. I loved to plunge my hand into the button bowl and let the buttons, all the colours and shapes and sizes of buttons, run between my fingers. I sorted them in rows and mixed them again. Sometimes I wish I had a big bowl of buttons.

THE CIGARETTE HOLDER

I have mentioned my uncle Llew. Pronounced Lou. His whole name was Jabez Llewellyn Bowering, but he was usually called "Red." He had a sign-painting business on Front Street, and a locally famous slogan: "Red's signs are read." Of course he had red hair, his wife Lorna from Seattle had red hair, and their son Russell had red hair. Uncle Red had a different mother from my dad's, and he looked a lot different from Ewart and Ella and so on. Heck, I'll mention that one year he was the underwater swimming champion of Seattle. They had an argumentative wire-haired terrier named Beans, who was mainly red-haired with white trim. It was at uncle Red's that I heard my first World Series game on his grand radio with the names of foreign cities on the dial. Cubs versus Tigers. I became a Tigers fan. Next year I became a Red Sox fan, and so I have been ever since. Uncle Red, I thought, was kind of swashbuckling, in a kind of small town suspender-snapping way. I think I remember that he had a straw boater hat and two-tone shoes in the summer. I know for sure that he had a horn-rimmed cigarette holder. As a boy I swore that I would never smoke cigarettes or drink alcohol, but I admired that snazzy cigarette holder. Tortoise shell? Uncle Red would often bite it so that it stuck upward, the way Franklin Delano Roosevelt did. In my grandparents' house there were two big heavy-framed pictures my uncle Red had painted years earlier, while he was recovering from a serious back injury, one of a St. Bernard dog's big face, and one of the stone house my grandparents raised their family in. I wish I knew where those paintings went, but I wish I had uncle Red's tortoise shell cigarette holder.

OBJECTS

Charles Olson announced that it might be a good plan to regard oneself as an object among objects, and in that way have a chance to share the secrets that objects know. To me that suggests not holding oneself as subject with the material about one and in one's poetry as objects, subject to one's gaze. Not to see something, compare it with something, and describe the independence out of it. Make the external internal and the internal external? Why? Why not let things do their own doings, not yours? Some thing such as a wooden hand gun has been living in my memory for a lot of years even though I know what psychologists might say it resembles or may become. If you know yourself as an object, you could be alert to your breath, your heart, your fingertips and your balance, all those things that are a little dicey for me at the moment. You may treat me as an object, as long as you treat me as well, in your hands or in your memory, as you treat the objects you have

15

the greatest affection or respect for. Just, please, do not seek to treat me as your subject. I had that as much as I could stand when I was still called a "British subject." Have a look at literature: when the subjective predominates you get bad news. See Ahab. Othello. Oedipus the King. So when I think about the objects in my memory I try to get them to be what they were. I am not on an analyst's couch or in a Tennessee Williams play. Description is an easy thing to do; not to describe throws you onto the resources that an object sensing itself must rely on and improve.

THE CRIBBAGE BOARD

Though my mother's father lived not that much farther away than did my father's parents, we hardly ever saw him. I thought it must be because the Brinsons were different from the Bowerings, or the Kootenays were not as handy as the Okanagan, though we used to live in between. Once in a while I see a picture of bulbous-nosed water-combed Emmitte Brinson playing marbles with me and my sister in her sun dress and I pass on to other things. But when my father's father-in-law fell on hard times, my father sold him our house in Greenwood for one dollar, as we were moving back to our own valley. When Granddad's wife died and he couldn't cope, I got four of his things: a little pair of bronze cowboy boots for a toothpick holder, a copy of Zane Grey's *Stairs of Sand*, something I don't remember, and a rat terrier named Dinky. I loved that dog with her fast little feet. She walked with me on my lone mountain hikes, brave little thing. In the summer at the orchard above Naramata, she spent whole days excavating groundhog tunnels. She had a habit of getting pregnant, as happened in small towns. But when I think of Granddad Brinson's stuff, what I think of most often is his cribbage board. I don't exactly remember him and my father playing crib on that board, but they must have. That's what men did when they weren't working. I'm pretty sure I learned to play on that board, and you know? I wish I had it now. Here's what it was — a deer antler with all the right holes in it, shaved flat on the bottom side. Imagine that yellowish brownish antler lying between two home-made-cigarette-smoking men who once in a while congratulated one another's pegging. That crib board has to be somewhere now.

THE BONE

My mother Pearl was brought up on a farm in the hills above Lake Okanagan, a generation away from the Ozarks. I've driven a rented car on a highway among the oak trees down there, sniffing for my DNA. There are two kinds of buildings alongside that highway — plain churches with large gravel parking lots, and gas stations where you can get something to eat, the only places where you can get something to eat. A few booths with yellow plastic tables and seats. The food consists of puzzling shapes that were deep fried earlier in the day. On the highway there is a lot of roadkill. I'm just saying. My mother, who died the night Donald Trump was elected U.S. president, never went down there. I often refer to my dear old mum as a hillbilly. She was really good at a lot of things, but she referred to China as "one of those places over there," and she was suspicious of feta cheese. So she was a bit superstitious. When I was a book-reading little boy, she had a Ouija board, and often invited in-laws and bridge club friends to sit around it with their fingers on it. I think she also went to séances, but I don't remember any at our house. She was a good athlete and kept herself trim until she was a bony 100-year-old who had only recently got her youngest son to do her income taxes. But superstitious. Always had a good look at her tea leaves. She told me that when she was a girl, years before she married at eighteen and gave birth to me at nineteen, she met a witch among the trees. The witch told her she'd be married three times. I think she stopped watching carefully in case of number three when she was in assisted living. The witch in the trees gave her a little round piece of bone and told her never to be without it. I hope it was with her when her body was burned.

THE TUBA

My pal Willy and I were strolling the hall at our high school, fine-tuning one of our new songs, when we were waylaid by Gar McKinley, saxophonist, dance-band leader and high school music teacher. He informed us that we were just the lads he was looking for. One does not want to hear these words from a teacher, so we were suspicious, but we decided to hear him out. If you fellows fill the positions I have available in the school band, I can guarantee that all eyes will be on you any time we are playing, marching or sitting, and in my experience you do seem to like that. And that is how Willy and I became the tuba section of the Southern Okanagan High School band. A year later Don Cranna joined us, and I assigned him the post of third bass. Soon he was playing quite a lot better than we were. Well, a lot of the time the work entailed an oomp and a pah, but when we came to the bridge in the "Colonel Bogey March" hitting the right notes and the notes right in time, but could we ever get loud! SOHS owned three tubas, one of which was a Sousaphone, the other two being regular massive double b-flat horns. SOHS was the last extravagant Art Deco school with separate gymnasium and theatre and greenhouses and music room built in British Columbia (1947, till a moron burnt it down early in the 21st century). The music room had tiered seating, and was shaped like a third of a pie, with soundproofing double doors. Getting a tuba, much less a Sousaphone, safely through those doors was a challenge. The Sousaphone and one of the other tubas were in pretty fair shape, but the third horn had a lot of dents and incisions around its widest part. We took turns on the instruments, but the bashed one was my favourite because of all the rattling and blaring its wounds added to the higher notes. A year later the school popped for another big horn, and when Morley Carter came to play it, I named him shortstop.

THE CANE

When I started carrying a cane, it was for looks. I should have had a straw boater, as my uncle Red may have had, and a checkered vest. Wear a moustache and a swagger. Canes run in the family. My father's father was a crip, shuffled down to Main Street and back with a crutch on one side and a cane on the other. I think uncle Red had a bamboo cane — at least he should have had, to go with his two-tone shoes. Two of the many things I found in our cellar were a pair of spats my dad had when he was a young rake with a Star two-door. I have a photo of my grandfather's great-grandfather William (1800-1880) holding a carved cane. My grandfather told me there were a hundred faces carved on that cane, which I can't tell for sure from the photograph of William holding it, but in any case, it was, Grandpa said, buried with its owner in the Thatcham graveyard. I've gone over there twice to stand over that grave and yearn. I have a carved (and painted) cane I bought somewhere in Mexico many years ago, but I don't walk with it any more. I have over the years acquired lots of those metallic drugstore canes you can fold up or telescope, and I usually keep a few in places where I need some help getting around. But my favourites are two oaken canes that my wife Jean bought for me by mail from Florida. One has a ¾-sized baseball for a handle, with real white leather and red stitching. I carry this one when we go to baseball games. But my favourite stick is beside me right now in Jalisco. Beautiful striped oak and brass, the handle that shape you've seen, made for the human hand. Once in a while I drop it with a clatter and the curved tip breaks off, where it has been glued back on I don't know how many times.

THE FROGS

Where there are objects there are collectors of objects. All my life I have been an on-again, off-again collector. Right after James Dean got himself killed on that California highway in 1955, four cheap one-issue pop magazines were published to cash in. I bought all four, including, because that is what we do, *Jimmy Dean Speaks from the Grave.* I still have them six decades later. Until recently I had boxes and boxes of baseball (and other sports) magazines from the forties and fifties, complete runs, of course. I do still have a complete run of Stan Lee's comic book about the Canadian superhero group *Alpha Flight*, including one Spanish translation. When I lived in a huge house in Kerrisdale, I had seven rooms of floor to ceiling books, but I sold or gave away thousands of them. The next house, in West Point Grey, was considerably smaller, and had only four and a bit rooms full of books. But we have moved to a condominium, and I have given away most of my books. Fortunately the nearby university library is making a space for the collection of books by the authors who mean most to me (H.D. and Robert Kroetsch, etc.) along with portraits of me by artists I dig, and objects I could not stop myself from cluttering my shelves with. Sometimes you get known for gathering certain objects, and people begin giving you some, often in taste you don't yourself possess, so you have to quit acquiring them and start giving them away. For many years, in emulation of a person I once met in the Niagara region, I collected frogs, mainly figurines. Two were once living toads in Latin America, later eviscerated and written upon. Another was a highly articulated frog-like creature fashioned of some light Asian wood. We kept it high on the back porch, where an uncooperative squirrel knocked it off its perch, and our big dog, who considered any such thing on the floor to be a chew-toy, finished it off.

THE CAMERAS

When I was a high school kid my buddy Willy and
I set up a darkroom under the stairs in the basement of
his house. So when I was an eighteen-year-old recruit
in the RCAF, I told them I'd like to be a cameraman.
They said finish first in the tests and you'll get your
choice. I did, and they sent me to trades training at
Camp Borden, Ontario, where I would become an
aerial photographer. It wasn't long until I was up in a
DC-3 with a camera the size of a washing machine.
Its lens looked through a hole in the fuselage floor,
and behind that was a roll of film eight inches wide
and two hundred and fifty feet long. The idea was
that the film would unwind as the plane moved,
and you would have a long photographic strip, of a
landing beach, for example. The eighteen-year-old
rookie was expected to coordinate the movement
of the film with the movement of the aircraft,
accounting for altitude, ground speed, drift, yaw, and
changes in any or all of these factors. I could do this.
After training there were postings we photographers
had to fill. I ranked first in tests again, but an older
guy took Comox, B.C. because he was married and

had a newly-born child. I could have grabbed P.E.I.-based Overseas Squadron, which spent half the year in the Caribbean. I chose the farthest west station, Macdonald, Manitoba, in snow country. It was an air gunnery training station for NATO student pilots. One day a French flyer pranged his T-33 jet through a bluff of little oaks. We had to send a photographer on the ground and another photographer by air. All the guys with stripes on their arms or shoulders were away from the photo section. LAC Bowering was in charge. Unfortunately all the aerial cameras were out, too. I had to make a military decision. I grabbed a Speed Graphic, the camera you see reporters photographing boxing matches in old black and white movies with. There I was, nineteen years old now, in the back of an Expeditor, headset connecting me with the pilot up front. We made a few passes above the wrecked kite, and I told the pilot to go down to 400 feet and bank sharp, because I had no telescopic lens. The men in the snow around the wreckage waved their hands, trying to shoo us. The Pratt & Whitney engines made an unpleasant sound. Eventually I pulled my head and camera back inside the opened doorway and said let's go home. If I had been a boy in the USAF, I would have been given a couple medals.

GADGETS

Nowadays eleven-year-old children on six continents are looking down at their hands and performing magic. With their little smart alec phones they can take photographs of microbes, order a Hawaiian pizza. Send intimate songs to their cousins on jet planes, and call for drone airstrikes to take out the enemy's basketball bus. The other day I saw a hirsute teenager using the haircut app. Do you remember the non-whiskered youth who performed like a high-wire Newton in the belly of an RCAF aircraft? Six decades later he is the victim of a conspiracy carried out by all the electric and electronic gadgets known to the overly modern world. Take that cell phone, for example. The airman who could calculate everything between his plane's yaw and his camera's focal plane is now lucky to wrest a readable photograph from his i6+ mobile. If I instruct it to send a text message to my daughter in another province, it is likely to inform me that something called "the cloud" is going to rain on my parade. I have had many home computers, and each one has been more difficult to plead with than its predecessor. I want it to be a nifty typewriter, but it wants to lift soil samples from Phobos, and the printer it whined for assails me with bright little exclamation marks. We have house phones all over the condo, but they baffle me. They make me long for 1956. Forget about the dashboard on our German sedan, much less the seat controls. Every appliance in the kitchen beeps at me and then eludes me, except for the digital clocks, which I can read — when they are correct. If I want to watch the Raptors game on channel six hundred and something, I ask my wife Jean to turn it on. I think I am a remote control someone gave up trying to show me how to use.

ROCKS

The largest object I've ever touched with my hand is our planet. Or with my feet or my imagination. On the north shore of Lake Erie, shortly before you run out of Canada, there is a grassy park that slopes down to the calm water. Below a tall deciduous tree there is a bench commemorating the short life of my stepdaughter Bronwyn. To the right of the bench is a plaque with a poem for her, and beneath it are some ashes becoming part of the largest object we have known. Also around the plaque are smaller objects — many rocks of various colours and shapes. Each of these rocks used to be somewhere else on the planet. There are rocks from Vancouver Island, Tierra del Fuego, Cuba, Alaska and India. There's a piece of volcano from Hawaii, a chunk of the Great Pyramid of Giza, and another from that other pyramid, the Temple of the Sun in Teotihuacan. The Great Wall of China is represented, as is the Acropolis.

I think that Bronwyn's mother Jean wished that Bronwyn could have gone and visited these sites, so she brought small bits of them to the park where she and her friends liked to hang out. In her luggage Jean carried pieces of Florida, Spain, Rome, Curaçao, and the Rocky Mountains. Some years ago Jean and I stayed in a house on the beach at the farthest north reach of the Yucatán peninsula, as close as you can get on foot to the site where the largest object ever to strike our planet crashed. Gathering special rocks from around the globe to place beside Bronwyn's bench is Jean's way of doing the opposite.

SHE WANTS TO BORROW MY COMB

When I was a junior high school kid, the boys that wanted to appear toughly snazzy kept rat-tail combs in a back pocket of their pants. Any time they wanted to, they could reach back, grab the handle, and get both hands on their long Brylcreem hair, one for dragging the comb through their ducktail, the other for smoothing. If you are old enough, you've seen that manoeuver a thousand times. A lot of people have stopped wearing watches because they now carry cell phones. Somewhere between my grandfather's generation and mine, men quit toting pocket knives, except in the Kootenays and parts of Nova Scotia. But just about everyone except Gregory Corso's ghost carries a comb. I can't honestly tell you when I started carrying one. I'm guessing it would be right after my mother quit spitting on her fingertips and gluing my kiss curl down. It is my mother's fault that I part my hair on the right. She said she couldn't remember which side boys parted it on. I have always carried my plain black comb in my right back pocket. Some guys, lefties especially, use the left back pocket. I think my uncle Red used to have his in his shirt pocket, along with his cigarette holder. Women, I suppose, keep theirs in their purses, along with those balled-up Kleenexes. But even in that short period when we guys carried shoulder purses, I always wore my comb on my ass. Do you let anyone borrow your comb? I thought of carrying another one in my left back pocket in case anyone asked. Oh, I just remembered. I carry my wallet in my left side pocket, just like Stephen Heighton, but I used to keep it in my right back pocket, so I kept my comb in my left back pocket. Plain black comb. If you are like me, you have a lot of them, and you don't know where they all came from. They seem to multiply, like shirt hangers.

HORSEHIDE

I guess my favourite object in the world is a baseball. When I was a kid, unlike the kids nowadays, I never held a white baseball. I don't think I ever had one that retained all 108 of its stitches. Of course, like any boy of my time, I wanted to know what was inside. My magazines and books told me that the centre was cork or gutta percha, unless that was a golf ball. Yes, I took one apart, but not because I was a well-off boy. Now I have baseballs all over the house. They accumulate faster and almost as mysteriously as combs. Once in a while I thin the collection, taking a bunch to baseball kids in Cuba or Mexico. Some, of course, they don't get, as for instance the one I threw to Milwaukee catcher Damian Miller in Miller Park before a game against Cincinnati. There's the foul ball that knocked Jean's glasses off in Reno. There's the one I threw out before the Niagara Stars' first ever Canadian League game in Welland in

2003. It was signed by catcher Rogelio Arias, and now lies in a bowl with the one Damian Miller autographed. A pure white baseball with no scuff marks, eh? With the name of the league on it. There was a time when big league baseballs were sewn by non-union women in the U.S. Then for a while they were made in Haiti so that Rawlings or whoever could pay workers 90 cents a day. Now, like just about everything else, they are made in China. My dog got hold of one of my baseballs and took it apart, stitch by stitch, the method she uses on her toy animals. All that is left of that baseball is one of the cowhide infinity shapes, you know what I mean? We still call a baseball the old horsehide, though they switched to cowhide decades ago. I like the sound of ball hitting bat or glove, but I did not like to hear the sound of a curveball coming through the air up high. I just love looking at a white baseball on one of my bookshelves, for example in front of the complete poems of Samuel Beckett.

AMONG OBJECTS

So an object is a thing, if tangible, placed before the eye, or if not tangible, before the mind. Let's say more or less solid items one can see and theoretically touch. Our planet's moon is a large object that few have touched, and that with the intermediary of space-age clothing. But now I have a junior grade philosophical question. Quite some time ago I had the lenses of my eyes cut away and replaced by artificial lenses. Leaving aside the qualities of objects seen through these lenses, can't we say that the artificial lenses were objects before they were attached to my eyeballs, and isn't there a problem in saying that they are now part of my subjective conglomerate? Of course you might interpose that every atom that makes up a human body came from our planet, and perhaps ultimately from stardust. Let's leave eyes for now, and consider teeth. The eyes might be part of the brain while teeth are the visible part of the skeleton. I have a question similar to the one above, as there is a row of artificial teeth screwed into my left lower jawbone and another in my right upper jawbone. Are these still objects? I mean, I don't consider my fingers and toes to be objects. Fifteen years ago a doctor in Welland inserted four short metal rods to hold my right hipbone together, and when I broke my right femur last spring, a Vancouver doctor took out those four short metal rods (I asked him whether I could have them for souvenirs, and he replied that the paperwork would be too much) and inserted a long metal rod in with the marrow, and some more connective pieces. I think that the airport metal detector would consider these rods to be objects, though they are not easily removable as are my hearing aids. But I can't use the airport metal detector because I have a defibrillator inserted under the skin of my breast, and it has wires whose ends are inserted into my heart. It also has a pacemaker to help it with the mathematics. I am probably not worth six million dollars in scrap, but I face the twenty-four dollar question: is it easier for me than for most people to follow Charles Olson's direction and sense myself as an object among objects?

THE RATTLE

In my house I have always had to have many *objets d'art*, along with *objets* that I merely said were *art*. Perhaps I am obtruding on this book's sequence properly entitled "Rooms," but the above noun insists. In any case, I cannot summon to memory the object I had last night planned for this morning. These *objets* are, if I may be a little fanciful, a small *musée* of my adult life at least. I have a black figure of Ganesh, for example, and even if I cannot always remember fully what he promises with all the objects in his numerous hands, I know enough to have him facing the entrance to our condominium. I don't know where he came from but I bought him in West Berlin in 1980. He rested heavily in the overhead compartments all the way home to Vancouver. Where there is a glass and wooden box with white sand inside and a broken Aztec bowl resting in the sand. I got this bowl from Laurette Sejourné in Mexico City in 1964. I also got the title for my novel about George Vancouver from her. In my mind the prominent piece of art in my "collection" is a painting titled *The Woolworth Rattle*, by Greg Curnoe. I bought it from Greg in 1967, and since then it has hung in an apartment in Westmount, two houses in Kitsilano, a house in Kerrisdale, a house in West Point Grey, and now in our condominium. It has also hung in Curnoe exhibitions in London Ont., Toronto, Ottawa, and Vancouver. I can't remember where it is going after my death. But that goes for me, too. There's a lot of terrific art where I live, and some of it you'd call *objets d'art*, and then there are a lot of *objets* that are a little this side of art. Take my Daffy Duck Pez dispenser, for example.

CUPS

Every morning one reacquaints oneself with one's usual objects — soap, razor, comb, toothbrush — and then the most important one of the morning, the coffee cup. Those readers who prefer to drink something nonsensical upon waking, such as tea or chocolate or vodka, can adjust and adapt here. If you're like me (and who would not be?), you'll have a choice among many cups, and some favourites. There are cups in your kitchen that you would never use; you would rather wash one of your favourites. This tells us something, doesn't it? Many years ago, when my chum Willy and I worked in his stepfather's plant, we would walk up to my family home and eat our lunch and drink coffee. Willy always used the pink cup with a mounted Mountie on it and a message on the bottom inside, that he could read only when he'd drained the coffee. It read, "Now back to work!" Every day upon reading this exhortation, Willy would groan his complaint and rise from his chair. One of the reasons I've always loved him. That cup is still, I think, among the dishes in our condominium, but the writing has been worn away. I would never drink my coffee from it anyway. In my study I have a cup that bears a photo of Willy grinning our famous Club grin. I used to drink coffee out of it, but since it developed a large triangular gap in the brim, I employ it to hold a lot of pens, most of which I will never use. I have just finished my morning coffee on the balcony of our winter rental on the southern coast of Jalisco, but I had to make do. I don't like any of the cups in this place.

UMBRELLAS

I spent most of my childhood in the Okanagan Valley, which is an irrigated desert, so I didn't get my hands on an umbrella. Then I got through four years in college and the air force, until I fetched up at the age of twenty-one at the University of British Columbia in Vancouver, also known as Rain City. With my background and prejudices I was of the opinion that umbrellas were for female people, so with no hat and an air force raincoat I tried to get by. Despite the fact that all my male friends who were brought up on the coast carried manly umbrellas as if it were the most acceptable usage, I did not relent till my second winter really set in. I acquired my first bumbershoot in the conventional way, as instructed by my male friends, marching in wet clothing to the lost & found counter at the campus bus stop.

"I've somehow lost my umbrella."

"Can you describe it?"

"Black, with a brown handle."

"Does this look like it?"

"No, it didn't have any broken parts."

"How about this one?"

"That's the fellow. Thank you."

Years later I would instruct my scholar daughter about rain protection on campus. Always, I said, leave with a better umbrella than the one you came with. Nowadays people such as I buy our inexpensive umbrellas at the drug store and retain them until the first rain squall turns them inside out. As I usually carry a cane bought at the drugstore, I have returned to my childhood ways, trying to keep my head, at least, dry with a wide-brimmed hat that I often have to save from the wind with the hand that is not holding my cane.

MY FAVOURITE OBJECT

I am a person who is always making lists.
Alphabetical lists, geographical lists, names of
authors, ballplayers, musicians, etc. I'm always
asking people, what's your favourite vegetable,
European city, song by the Coasters. My favourite
European town is Plovdiv, favourite colour is
yellow, favourite poet is Shelley. But this is not a
book about favourites; that may come later, you
lucky people; it is a sequence about objects. All
right, what is my favourite object in the world?
Let me tell you something. I was a Protestant
boy in a family where people didn't hug one
another. I had to learn late to tell anyone how I
felt about anything. Yes, I have spent a lot of my
life exposing myself to the fine arts, but I don't
make a practice of blubbering about beauty. All
right. On three occasions I have wept and nearly
fallen down when presented with a work of art.
One happened in Montreal, where I was listening
to a poetry reading by George Oppen. Another

was at the Chan Centre at UBC, where for the first time I heard 80-year-old Ornette Coleman play live. The third, and it was in no sense third, occurred when for the third time I stood close and beheld my favourite object in the world. I will not attempt to describe it to you. Its beauty and force and divine origin make it live beyond the reach of description. I am referring to Donatello's *Magdalena*. A ragged, suffering haunted woman made out of wood. Out of. I won't try to tell you what the experience is *like*. See a photograph, a computer image. No, go there, to the Works of the Duomo in Florence. It was in a different location in the building each time I saw it. When you have spent an hour looking at it, go up the street and see Michelangelo's big marble *David*, to return to earth.

LUCK

"Objects in the mirror are closer than they appear." There's a philosophical proposition that has bothered me more and more as I see it again and again. People sometimes call me a rear-view mirror guy because I would feed the dictionary into the fireplace fire if it told me that "imply" and "infer" were interchangeable. I say focus tighter. The objects are not in the mirror; they are reflected by the mirror. I suppose that the manufacturer is trying to avoid accidents. If that is so, he should not be encouraging loose usage. Perhaps he should note the difference between "appear" and "seem to be." If I am sitting in the front passenger seat of the automobile in question, the image in the mirror may be less than an arm's reach from me, while the object behind us, presumably another automobile, is a few car lengths behind us. In other words, the object, which is not in the mirror, where it could do us little harm, but following the object in

47

which we are riding, is not closer than its image in the mirror, but still close enough to kill us if its driver or ours is careless enough not to keep at least one eye on the road behind or in front of us. Naturally, if our driver is driving in reverse gear, as when backing into a parking spot, the objects not in but reflected by the mirror may be closer to the back of his car than he or a careless mirror manufacturer might wish. Any passenger might be forgiven for wondering why the last-mentioned person could not find a way to make a mirror that reflects distances more accurately. In that way he might prevent instances of bad luck that continues for seven years.

FOOD

Tell me what you eat, and I will tell you
what you are.

> – Anthelme Brillat-Savarin,
> *Physiologie du Gout*

TOAST

My mother had a blue budgie to whom she gave the run, or rather the flight, of the house. Billy spent a lot of his time in front of a mirror that used to be a window in the front room. But if you tried to butter your toast quietly in the kitchen you would nevertheless hear the flutter of wings, and a blue flash would alight close to or on the edge of your slice. Toast was Billy's favourite food, and it is now our dog's favourite food, and our friend Guido's favourite food. In her old age my mother had to be talked into eating anything else. In our family we had seen pop-up toasters in the cartoons and the movies, but we had the regular kind, with doors that opened downward on either side. When the slices were done on one side you'd open the door and turn the slices over. Usually one side would get burned black, and you would scrape the black off with your knife before slapping on the butter. Then Billy would come like a Spitfire around the doorway. In our family, once you got your slice of hot toast (except in our grandparents' place, where they kept the British custom of letting your toast get cold and hard in a little ceramic toast rack. After they died, we put the toast rack in the goldfish bowl for scenery) you chose butter or jam as something to spread on it. No one in our family employed the benighted practice of spreading peanut butter on toast. My grandmother, who liked telling me stories of the funny things her youngest son, my uncle Gerry did, told us that he got around the rule by putting butter on one side of his toast and jam on the other.

APPLES

On Halloween there were a few people who asked us in and made us sing for our treats, so Willy and I had a routine, a song that ended "Kellogg's is the food for I," at which we would slip from our pose of leaning on each other's palms. Then there was the cheap son of a bitch who gave us an apple instead of candy. Come on! When my family first moved back to the Okanagan Valley, we lived in the house of an army officer who had moved his family to England. We had food hanging from trees all around us, just like everyone else. Cherries, apricots, peaches, pears, prunes, peachplums, and apples. After moving into town, we always had a box of apples in the cellar. The back yard had corn and raspberries and peas and beans and so on, and the front yard was full of potatoes. And there were chickens pecking away here and there. The Red & White store and the Overwaitea store were for flour and corn flakes and coffee. If I ever said, being a teenage boy, that I was hungry, my father, who grew up in orchards, said, "Eat an apple." It still feels funny buying a few pieces of fruit in a supermarket or greengrocer's. We got our boxes of fruit from uncle Gerry or the orchard my father and I were working in. Buying a little fruit, I thought, would be like paying money for pieces of gravel. But here's something I *would* pay money for: learning how to do what some orchard veterans, including my father, could do — pick up an apple and break it in half in your hands.

TOMATOES

Here is the way my father ate Shredded Wheat. He boiled some water in the kettle, then used his spoon edge to damage the top of the shredded wheat biscuit, then held the biscuit with his spoon while he poured a little hot water to soften it. Then he used the spoon to cut a groove lengthwise in the softened biscuit, and filled the groove with brown sugar. He did all this to avoid milk. My father didn't like milk. I don't know why — maybe because it had been in a cow. Maybe it was something between him and his mother. He also refused to eat tomatoes. Is there anything less like milk? And this in the southern Okanagan Valley, where yummy beefsteak tomatoes are so big that one slice serves for a large tomato sandwich, along with lots of mayonnaise — Joe Brainard's favourite. When I was a boy I decided that tomatoes were one of my four favourite (I keep bringing up favourites) foods, the others being cheese, eggs and onions.

Of course, living where I lived, and in the family I had, I didn't know that there were any cheeses other than orange mouse cheese. Nowadays my favourite is manchego, the great Spanish sheep cheese, the harder the better. Tomatoes, cheese, eggs, and onions. Without knowing it, I was an Italian boy! My home town looked and felt like the Mediterranean, according to the cliché one was always hearing. I have always maintained that after his week's work was done God asked himself what would make humans truly happy. The answer came: onions! All the variations of onions. Chives, shallots, leeks, garlic, scallions, red onions, white onions, yellow onions. Walla Walla sweets. And eggs? When the breakfast waiter asks me how I would like my eggs, I say, "One shirred and one pickled." And what can you do with a tomato? Don't ask my father; ask an Italian.

PICKY EATERS

My father was not the only picky eater in my family. My sister wasn't fond of meat, so here's how she ate her supper: separate the parts, eat the vegetables (usually carrots or string beans) first, then the potatoes, finally the chicken or beef or whatever. Make sure that once on the plate, none of these things is touching any other. Eat the meat in tiny pieces. My father made up for this tidiness by roiling everything together in one awkward stew. When my kid brother got old enough to have a plate at our table, the list of things he thought he could not eat was remarkably long. If he ever had spaghetti, which most kids like better than anything else, it could have nothing on it but butter and salt. The first time he ever saw a pizza, he knew he would detest it, until one day in his late forties he somehow gave the Greek special a try, and spent the remaining years of his life with the three pizza joints' telephone numbers prominent on his refrigerator door. When the pizza arrived he would scrape the olives onto someone else's slice before shoving the triangle into his mouth. As for my mother, she had a fear of exotic foods, such as feta cheese and bell peppers, so her pickiness was seen (or not seen) in the absence of anything unusual in the grocery bags that found the way to our kitchen. When my other kid brother showed up he fashioned a list as long as our middle brother's. When I was a boy I was even more exclusionary than the person who bought our food and cooked our meals. The list of vegetables I liked was shorter than the list of vegetables I would not try, and this list would of course not include the vegetables my mother was wary about buying. Now in my old age I am trying to eat a lifetime's supply of spinach, cabbage, turnips, kale, zucchini, parsnips, squash, vegetable marrow, okra and beet tops. As a boy I could not swallow chicken because I knew it when it was alive, and I could not chew anything from the sea or even a lake. I nearly committed suicide when my mother brought finnan haddie to the table.

DRUMSTICKS

When you are in the hospital, you discover that you have lost your appetite when the people with plastic hairnets bring your tray of something foodlike three times a day, generally a few hours earlier than your usual meal times. Once, when I was in Vancouver General Hospital after a cardiac arrest, my first meal by mouth consisted of a dawn breakfast in which all the ingredients were puréed, including cold toast and strawberry jam. After a few days you find yourself tasting more than a spoonful of porridge and milk, and after a few weeks you surprise yourself by eating the whole little bowl of it. In recent times the kitchen has been sending a person to take one's requests for next day's meals. "Would you like salmon sandwich or fish sticks for lunch," etc. One day I checked under the heavy plastic dome and around it, to learn that in every instance I got b. where I had ordered a. with my heart oozing hope, drumstick instead of pork chop, spice cake instead of apricots, etc. But after a month you find that you just clean up whatever they drop in front of you. Those vegetables you could not identify become your trusted fare. I remember a pregnant alley cat I once adopted. I relocated her from a West End industrial lane to a tony neighbourhood in Kerrisdale. For her new diet I offered her the cat kibble my other cats resolutely consumed. For days she would not touch it, but before the week was out she was crunching it and protecting it from the other cats. She did not forego her former ways entirely. Once I saw her returning from an excursion down our alley with a big rectangle of salmon skin hanging from her jaw. Now, I am not a willing consumer of fish skin, but toward the end of a hospital stay I will be cleaning my plate and ordering a. for the next day.

RAJITAS

My third dental implant surgery was a little complicated; for some reason, it involved skinning my palate and swinging that skin over to the right half of my upper jaw, where the drilling and implanting were to take place. I've endured a lot of operations, so this was just another minor horror. My palate is not now as smooth as it once was. A few years later I experienced a cardiac arrest, after which I was in an induced coma for two weeks. I don't remember, thank goodness, but I had some tied-together hoses or the like shoved down my throat to reach whichever organs they were designed for. My dental hygienist told me that the surfaces of my tongue and mouth were no longer bubbly, but now smooth and purplish. That change has brought me one of the unhappiest alterations in my personal experience of eating. Until the age of old fogeyism, I enjoyed and bragged about eating every variety of spicy food, especially Mexican, Indian, and Thai. One 1964 evening in San Angel, Coyoacan, Mexico City, my pal the poet Lionel Kearns and I engaged in a historic rajita-eating contest at el Coyote Flaco, a wonderful Mexican restaurant. Rajitas are kind of like pickles, except that they are menacingly hot. In pure cooking they are supposed to be roasted and sliced chiles, mostly poblanos, but when you see a little side dish with them in it, they will be accompanied by very hot pickled slices of carrots, onions, and other vegetables. At el Coyote Flaco they were available to any of the diners, including the evil poet Sergio Mondragon, whose idea this all was. Of course Lionel and I had to exhibit our worse *machismo*. "I can eat all these *cascabeles!*" "I can eat all these gentle-looking carrots!" It is probably considered rude to lie on the floor, red-faced in a classy restaurant, tears all over your face. Oh, I miss those days. With my smooth tongue's surface, I can no longer gobble satisfyingly hot food. My bragging days are gone. I ate butterscotch pudding tonight.

PIE

For my eighth birthday, when we were living in an orchard two miles south of town, my mother gave me a choice: would I like her to bake me a cake, which I understood to be traditional, or an apple pie, which I figured to be quite unusual. Though I felt the semi-obligation to cleave to tradition, I really did like pie better than cake, so I declared my individuality by opting for pie. Then my twenty-seven-year-old mother pulled one of her Protestant tricks. She asked me which I would prefer: to have the pie all to myself, or to share it with my parents and sister. Well, of course I wanted to eat the whole thing; I was, after all, a reader of *The Katzenjammer Kids*, and admired their attraction to the hot pie left on the cooling windowsill by the Captain's wife. But I knew what my mother wanted for an answer. I replied, as much as if I meant it as I could manage, that I preferred to share the pie. Remember, all this is in the context of my mother's manifest skill in the making of a pie, whether apple or cherry or mince. Oh, well, let me just list some of the pies she excelled at producing and which made me glad I was living within her purlieu: peach, peach and pear, apricot, blackberry, raisin, huckleberry, the divine saskatoon, lemon, red currant, chokecherry, rhubarb and strawberry, and all those ones that were not really pie — chocolate, Boston creme, banana crème, coconut crème and butterscotch — puddings with a bottom crust, really. What a world I lived in in the forties, where most of the things my mum made pie from were hanging in trees surrounding our house. But when she made cinnamon baked apples for dessert, well, that wasn't pie, either. And it was a little like getting an apple in your Halloween swag.

COMICS FOOD

Greg Curnoe and I must have been meant to be soul mates, and I know that he would have guffawed at the word soul. So, not soul and not mates, except in the Australian usage. For example, we both liked collecting things, as boys and as adults, and as boys we found our beginnings in comic books and newspaper funnies, he as artist and I as writer. I liked a lot of things about the comics — how hair-gooed hair was drawn as a shiny reflecting part of a head of hair, for example. And for another example, the way comics characters were characterized by the foods they favoured. Anthelme Brillat-Savarin could have been a cartoonist. Probably the most famous comics food was the hamburger that Wimpy was always yearning for. I was reading about Wimpy's yen when I had never seen hamburgers because I was a kid in small towns where they didn't exist. Years later, after I had gone to Victoria to attend college, I would sing a jukebox song called "That's Amore," and though I knew what *amore* was, I had no notion what a "peetsa" might be. Sometimes comics food was a bit like superhero magic, so that while Billy Batson might exclaim "Shazam!" Popeye would swallow a can of spinach before going into action. Well, we all knew what Etta Candy had a weakness for. I envied Archie's treating Veronica to a soda, not because I wanted to make headway with Veronica, but because being a small-town Canadian, I had never had or seen a soda. The best we could ask for was a "float," which consisted of a scoop of ice cream plopped into a tall glass of Pepsi. I always wanted to see what the Invisible Scarlet O'Neil ate, because I wanted to see whether we could see some chewed food before it became part of her. But probably our most heroic eater was Dagwood Bumstead, who could somehow walk from fridge to table with food items from hands all the way up to his shoulders. What kid my age never fixed himself a Dagwood sandwich?

POTATOES

When I was a wee chappy, a little plump and smiley, I was the potato boy. I knew that potatoes were ordinary, a toss-in, not high on the glamour scale, but I even loved the way my dad said "spuds" or "taters." I loved boiled potatoes with butter and parsley and salt, my favourite. Well, really, my favourites were pan-fried potatoes, nice and crisp and maybe a little burnt. I'd never heard of other kinds of fries until as a young grown-up (seventeen) I went to Victoria and had some English chips in a cone of newspaper, and now I forlornly look for them everywhere, haven't had any for all of my old age, not even when I sought them in London, don't want to make do with so-called French fries, most of which have been frozen. But really, my favourites were the potatoes that were cooked with onions around an oven roast. Once, visiting home when I was youngish, I ate eleven, having warned my amused mother to make lots and lots. But what about mashed potatoes, every kid's favourite, with or without gravy, maybe a river of butter flowing down a mountain of mashed or creamed potatoes, or if we were at Grandma's, riced potatoes, one of the reasons for looking forward to visiting her. But I haven't mentioned baked potatoes, cut them in half and apply butter and sour cream when we could finally get that, and salt and pepper, don't even bother with scissored green onions and some kind of bacon bits. I tried for years to get my father to eat his potato skins. In later years the wonderful way the Germans make shaved potatoes in the oven, the Italians and Austrians can show you a thing or two, the Greeks with their lemon flavouring. But, okay, here's my real favourite — scalloped potatoes, even without cheese, but better with. The cream, the sacred onions, the crust on top that you try to get more than your share of. Wait! Did I forget something?

CHICKEN

There were two words I would habitually doodle in the margins of my scribblers while listening to a professor talk or to someone on the telephone. These were "yes" and "chicken." I am not a psychologist, so I don't know why. Now I just tell people that "chicken" is my favourite word. I especially like the sound of it, and so does our dog. When I was a boy everyone had chickens in the yard. These, of course, were not pets, and they were not the few you needed for eggs. They were backyard meat on yellow legs. I don't even remember whether you could go to a grocery store and buy a chicken breast or drumsticks or, heaven forbid, wings. When it was time for a chicken dinner, my father would add a little more blood to the chopping block, then after the headless yardbird quit running, he would hand it over to my mother. First she would submerge the unlucky hen in a bucket of boiled water. I detested the odor that resulted, I did not volunteer to do the plucking, especially while I could hear the surviving birds clucking. I could not imagine my mother and my father raising turkeys or rabbits. After all the feathers were out, leaving dots where they had been, and that blue-skinned bird was on its back on the newspaper on the kitchen table, I guess my mother slit its bottom open, because soon I saw her pulling all the yellow and purple stuff that came sliding out. I could see the several *parts*, and so could the cats that were looking in the kitchen window. The odour now was preferable to the feather smell, but only just. Now my mother was doing what needed doing with string and checking the stove for wood. I hadn't said a word, and my mother knew why. I was the boy who had the job of feeding this chicken, and I had often reached under her for an egg. I was thinking about how recently she was pecking at the ground out there, and I was not going to eat her. My mother expected me to outgrow such reluctance.

MEATLOAF

In my current marriage I don't seem to do any of the real cooking. Well, I'm responsible for finding my breakfast and lunch, but Jean treats me to a yummy dinner around 8 p.m. most nights. Including a glass of red wine. She never makes me a meatloaf, any real man's favourite dinner, but takes care of me when it comes to the ingredients I need. Such as potassium and vitamin K. My previous wife was a good cook, but in the later part of our marriage, I did just about all the cooking. Well, no one is going to maintain the fake news that I was a sophisticated cook. Many of my dishes were organized around ground beef. In my defence, if I need one, I'll say that I usually selected extra lean ground beef. Yes, of course I made meatloaves. First I fried (or as we chefs say, sautéed) chopped onions in butter — no, wait, I think that was the start of my spaghetti sauce. Anyway, I chopped up a lot of onion and put it in a mixing bowl with the raw meat, then poured in a raw egg or two, some vinegar or wine, lots of ground pepper, salt (back when it was okay to use salt), ketchup, HP Sauce, Worcester Sauce, maybe some halved stuffed olives, sugar, maybe brown, half a handful of breadcrumbs, some kind of bottle chile, etc., etc. , use hands to mush it all together, enjoying the egg yolk's slithering over the back of your hand, then transferred the lot to a loaf pan. Get it in there, I've forgotten some stuff, then cover the top with ketchup and mustard, the yellow kind. Sometimes instead of that I would use orange marmalade on top — that's a trick I learned from Carol Matthews, who also taught me in Westmount, Quebec that you can bake little meatloaves in muffin tins. Oh, yes, if you have some capers in the fridge, especially the big ones, they go nicely, and if you are making picadillo, which my daughter didn't like much, you can add raisins.

WILLY'S SANDWICHES

My buddy Willy and I had a lot of neat routines when we were kids and then youths. There was the "Uncle Louie" routine, for instance, and the "oh, there you are!" routine or the "once when I was young I was down in a coal mine" routine. These were brief routines, designed to entertain bystanders. We had active routines that did not require an audience, as for example, telephoning the office if we saw a sign that read "Telephone Office." You can imagine what transpired when a sign enjoined, "Wet Paint." Here is one that in our dotage we still talk about, pondering the wisdom of starting it up again after a recess of sixty years. This routine was usually performed with a very limited audience, or none at all. Willy would say in a loud and formal tone, "I guarantee to eat any sandwich you make." This boast was an extension of our boyhood drama about the importance of food to Willy's life. Usually we performed this routine in my mother's kitchen (as we said in those days) when my mother was away from the house. The rule was that I could construct the sandwich out of any food in the house, if said food was not locked up or hidden away. Because I wanted to challenge my buddy's boast, I would of course conjoin items not often tasted together — mustard and grape Jell-O, for example. I must say that I was deeply impressed by Willy's courage, though as president of our Club I enforced a founding law that if I accepted his invitation to try a bite, we would be breaking the rules of the contest. Naturally, I cannot recall all my creative combinations, but I will never forget Willy's difficulties with the sandwich I built on a base of sardines and Scotch mints.

LUNCH AT DUINO

One time in Bologna, I mentioned to a waiter that people often mention France when the topic of conversation turns to cuisine. "See?" I said, "even the word we use for it is from the French." The waiter picked up my empty artichoke plate and replaced it with a little bowl of *sopa all'Imperatrice*. "Yes," he said, "the French may know something about cooking, but they know nothing about eating." There was a wonderful Italian stress on that last word. And I know, as we say over here, where he was coming from. I have eaten more meals in Italy than I have in France, and as anyone who has seen an Italian movie knows, the Italians are indeed the champions of the big family dinner at a deal table outdoors. I have to say that in 1966, I had one of my great culinary trips as Tony Bellette and I drove in a new Volkswagen Beetle around eastern France, We stopped at rural inns and ate country food, starting each evening with a tureen of soup this

Campbell's-raised boy had never dreamed of. But we were only travellers, and years later I was just a visiting "scholar" when I joined a bunch of French professors for lunch, a mid-day dinner in a downstairs restaurant somewhere near the Sorbonne, or Paris VI, as we academics called it. Years later this "scholar" fulfilled a long-lasting ambition by visiting Duino Castle, where Rilke penned two of his eponymous elegies. Before entering the fabled site Jean and I had an *al fresco* lunch outside a nearby restaurant. Saying hello to the dozen people, children and grandparents included, at a long table in the shade of some scant black pines, we spent an hour and a half there while Jean consumed some creatures fresh from the Adriatic, one of which had black eyes at the ends of long stalks. Two hours later, when we came back out of the castle, that family was still there, perhaps having some Triestine coffee.

COMFORT FOOD

When you were a child you developed a taste for one or more comfort foods, and now that you are an adult, and perhaps even old, you retain the yen for that comfort food. This is one of the main ways you connect with your own childhood. Everyone knows what comfort food is. For one thing, it is the opposite of fine cuisine. I think it is related to the cravings that pregnant women get. Some of those are bizarre, such as sardines with Scotch mints, say. But most of the regular comfort foods I have been told about I would feel comfortable eating up. For instance, Kraft Dinner. Every kid loves that low-class pasta, those little macaroni elbows with some kind of orange-coloured cheese-like product. Some kids don't put ketchup on theirs, but most of us do. Some years ago Kraft tried putting powdered ketchup in the box along with powdered cheese-like product, but it was a big failure. They keep trying things like white cheese-like product or funny-shaped pasta, but really, you should not fool around with multi-generational comfort food. Well, you can throw some frozen peas in with the pasta while it is being boiled. When I ask friends about their favourite comfort foods, I often hear about KD. Mine used to be breakfast cereal, especially Raisin Bran. In our family we used to have a bowl of breakfast cereal before going to bed. I think that people are sometimes ashamed of their comfort food. I know that I have a twinge of shame-like feeling when I open a can of pork and beans. Here's what a lot of people my age tell me: tomato soup and a grilled cheese sandwich. I know of three poets from Tulsa who hankered for Pepsi-Cola. When I asked my friend Lynn, she hesitated, then confessed, "Peanut butter on a finger."

VERDE, BLANCO, ROJO

My two favourite foods, as in cuisines, are Italian food and Mexican food. Cooks in both countries like to make dishes that present the colours of their flags. Both flags are green, white and red, and you are likely to eat some pasta that is green, white and red, or consume a plate of food that features hot salsa verde, hot salsa Colorado, and cooling sour cream. I have twice been to restaurants in Italy that were billed as "Mexican," one in Florence and one in Verona. In both cases the fare was somewhat more like a Mexican dinner than it was like an Inuit breakfast — but in one case it was pitiable, and in the other it was vile. In Mexico I have ordered an Italian dish a few times. Each time it was not particularly vile, but it made a person think: why would I want to eat this when there's a perfectly acceptable *cochinita pibil* on offer in the next block? One good test of a country's cooking is whether you'll ever get tired of its street food or homely café stuff. Personally, I don't need to have sushi more than once a quarter, and anything made of chickpeas gets a little wearing on its way to the table sometimes. But as any four-year-old will tell you, you can live for months on pasta as long as the noodles keep changing shape. In Mexico there are dozens of things that offer delight inside a tortilla or poured over it. If you were to drive from Genoa to Trieste, taking your time and treating your tummy, you would find that each city along the way can teach you something interesting about risotto. If you happen to fetch up in Mérida during your Yucatán travels, you might abstain from food all day and then have a huge dinner at la Chaya Maya. Don't skip dessert.

SWEET TOOTH

It's one of those words or phrases I always heard when I was a kid, and never understood: "a sweet tooth." My mother had one, modified by her deprived upbringing, and I remember her using the term more than anyone else. I mean she and my sister used to have butter and sugar sandwiches. My mother put sugar on half the things she ate. Sweet tooth. It was a puzzling adult expression, like the one used by my Baptist grandmother, who wanted to know whether I had had a bowel movement that day. I didn't know what she meant nor why she was interested. I hadn't felt my bowels moving; I knew that. So sweet tooth. Weren't we talking about the hankering for something sweet to sink our teeth *into?* I had a semi-deprived childhood, certainly by today's expectations, but when I think back on it, my childhood did include enough sweets to involve favourites, say. Often I had to be inventive to get what my, well, not teeth but mouth anyway, desired. For example, when I was maybe twelve, I knew a never locked window in one of the fruit-packing houses, and there I went, thence to the pop cooler (you remember the ones filled with cold water), where I retrieved just one, often Mac's lime or Mac's grape, and then went back through the window to the dark. I knew the thrill of the intruder who could have been nabbed by the very figures he cheered for in the comic books he read. Or there was, in a less criminal way, the method by which Willy and I got a brick of ice cream. If you took a dozen empty beer bottles down to some garage across from the tracks, they gave you twenty-five cents for them. Willy's dad had a lot of cases of empties in their basement. Then at the grocery store a pint brick of ice cream was priced at twenty-five cents. They would chop the still-packaged ice cream in two, and give us two little wooden spoons, and off we would go. If my mother had only known! Okay, I still have a bit of a sweet tooth, and I still associate it with a bit of sneaking.

BALLPARK FRANKS

If you travel the world in search of baseball games, you are not going to be able to avoid ballpark food. People talk about ballpark food whenever their conversation turns to the subject of ball parks. There are three main topics in these conversations. One, the terrible high prices of the hotdogs and beer and so on. Two, the poor quality of the food as compared to the same stuff you could have at home. And three, the outrageous specialty items for sale at particular stadiums. Just for an example, I will not name the park in which you can get a hamburger containing four patties of some meat, along with four slices of cheese plus onions, tomatoes, lettuce, mustard, ketchup, mayo, chiles, and rather than a simple hamburger bun, a halved giant-sized Krispy Kreme doughnut! Don't worry, I am not going to list all the atrocious culinary insults to be found, not even the turkey leg that Jean bought at a Lakeland Flying Tigers game. It was as big as her head, and the universal rule applies inside or outside a ball park: never eat anything bigger than your head. Sometimes the fare at the stadium is what you might expect, given the geography. Hence, you will get clams and sushi in Seattle — but what explains the other notable option there? I'm talking about crickets. But at heart, baseball food comprises hotdogs, popcorn, and peanuts. Once, during a persistent drizzle, I saw a baseball game played at a hillside park just outside Basel. As you might expect, the quality of the baseball playing was nothing to text home about — but this was Switzerland; I had the best ballpark hotdog ever! But let's go from Switzerland to its opposite. They have always loved baseball in Saskatchewan, but it's the prairies, eh? We once went to a playoff game in Moose Jaw. The ballpark food came on a paper plate. It consisted of roast turkey, mashed potatoes with gravy, and mixed veg.

A LITTLE LUNCH

A little cheese on my father's thumb. Here Here and Here along a celery branch. And I didn't tell him for years. It took some effort, making food fun for the kid. There was no Whiz. There was no Whiz in school lunches. Real cheddar hard pressed into place so selfish and so pure. Black marker on white egg is so nice to look at. I showed everyone. Various expressions for hard boiled. My father's faces birdfoot eyes laughing to tears, sometimes. Sometimes a surprised looking Banana. Something every day from brown paper. And thrown away. Sadly, no one wants to eat a thumb print. No one much wants to crack or peel a face, either. What was left? A suitable sandwich? I don't remember. I remember what is thrown away. Which is the same as what is eaten. My mother made cucumber sandwiches with no crusts and called it a Little Lady Lunch. I don't remember eating them and she's not here. Somewhere my father compares a good book to a good meal. I could look that up. You don't remember the details. You remember the feeling of eating it. I never ate the celery with the abused cheese in it. When I was a little girl I tried hard to understand a poem about lemons, and one about plums, and a poem my father wrote about blackberries: it was white type on dark blue, a strip of green at the top, the title dark blue inside the green, a card pinned to a cork board in my room. I looked at it every night from bed. I'm looking at it now. Every week after the piano lesson we went to the Dairy Queen and my father ordered a milkshake with real blackberries in it. He got mad at me for ordering a root beer milkshake when I could have gotten one with real fruit. But why struggle? A root beer shake is a rare thing too, I said. And delicious. I was afraid to tell. But years later when I did my dad laughed and was delighted. He tells the story of the kid every day throwing away the cheese and celery with his thumbprint in it.

– Thea Bowering

FOOD ALLERGIES

When my daughter was a toddler, she was allergic to milk and anything containing milk, lactose intolerant we called it, and to gluten and anything made of wheat. You will have to imagine how difficult it was to throw a birthday party, especially with a rice flour cake with rock-solid icing. Remember that expression "It's a phase she's going through — she'll grow out of it"? Apparently, it can apply to physical health, thank goodness. If you are like most people, you have never heard of an allergy to sage. I found out about it when I cooked a pork chop for my sweetheart Jean. When we go to friends' places for Christmas or Thanksgiving turkey, our host makes a second kind of stuffing for Jean. I do not anymore desire to see my life's partner as a conduit. Ironically, where I grew up the most prolific wild plant life is sagebrush. Smells nice. Some allergies are embarrassing. Some can make a person too ill to go to a poetry reading. A marvellous poet I know wears a gas mask whenever she rides in an airplane, because now that the airlines make their passengers bring their own food on board, there's a much greater likelihood that someone will have brought peanuts or something made of peanuts. Lethal snacks and oblivious travellers make an unfortunate combination. Then there are my married friends Cara and Chuck. They are allergic to just about any foodstuff you can name. My dog eats corn on the cob daintily though eagerly, but Chuck cannot abide anything made of any part of corn, which in the USA, for example, is just about anything. When you have Cara and Chuck over for dinner, you'd better be serving kale and peaches with a mild chicken foot sauce.

WHAT? ALREADY?

I think I know why we always had breakfast
cereal before we went to bed in our family. It
was because dinner (called supper in our house
because dinner was the noon meal) was served
at five, or shortly after. Years later, my sister and
her husband always had a snack or really another
lunch-like meal late at night, by which I mean
around ten, because they had supper at five if not
before. That is also what old-timers did in the
assisted living place where my mother lived for
some of her long old age. At 4 p.m. you would see
people sitting around as close as they could get
to the dining room, waiting out the minutes till
supper time. I guess a lot of them used to live an
agricultural life, quickly putting away a 5 o'clock
meal before heading back to the orchard to work
till it got dark. I did a lot of orchard work when
I was young, and I never got to like it. Over the
last three years I have had three longish hospital
stays, and I didn't like the meals all that much

there. As we have seen, there are two things to be known about hospital meals: they come too early and they don't taste all that good. (Though they wear you down: after a month in VGH and UBC Hospital last spring I was eating everything that arrived on my tray. It always came with a little print-out telling you what the things on your tray were.) Breakfast arrives before the sun does. Lunch gets to your bed before the hour hand points straight up, and guess what? 5 o'clock. Except on weekends, I was reminded last month. On the weekend, dinner will be there at 4:30. Four. Thirty. About four hours before you usually have your evening meal, *n'est pas?* Look around any hospital ward — you will find food items stashed away for the long p.m.

SALAD

It is a winning cake, someone said. This winning is because of the ingredients. Stirring is not everything. There will always be an end to stirring. But dropping. You can think clearly while dropping and you are not a tree. The leaves come from our knees kneeling. A winning cake is no contest though they try to make it one, like sashes and not like salad dressing. Food often involves participles, like no contest. Please an artichoke in French or Italian, a thistle not a sound. Keep trying to keep up with your imaginary eyesight. The text could always be this way we could any time drop what we are doing, like leaves. We had a salad before we were married. We walked in tight pants across that province and this one. Was it a cake walk, I don't know, what is a cake walk? Cocoa and clear soup and oranges and oatmeal. She is always telling me to eat this and that, and that is always salad and I hope it is salad with avocado and potassium. Potatoes are our favourites, this one and that other writer. Potatoes are seldom in a salad but then potatoes are a salad. When I was a boy eleven years old my favourite colour was green, but exactly the green you saw on the egg carton now it is yellow and yes sometimes there is yellow in the salad more often when it is a winning cake. Red tulips and yellow daffodils beside the black dog so much depends upon see another chapter. I chose pie over cake but now under a wise and heavy influence I choose salad almost every time.

GETTING OLD

It used to be that you just ate what your mum made for dinner, trying to take as many spuds as you could and eating as little in the way of turnips as you could get away with. Same thing with more nervousness when you were at Auntie Pam's when you worked there, or at Auntie Jennie's when you went to college and weren't allowed to read at the table. Then whatever you wanted, including, one Christmas day, a full plate of olives. Then at university you ate whatever you got for sixty-five cents at the Varsity Grill, or whatever the better-off students left on the trays they didn't bother putting away at the cafeteria. You went for years eating whatever there was. Later you got married and had some really nice meals and learned to eat stuff you'd never eaten before, and after a while you did the cooking and it wasn't all that fancy but you got as much meatloaf as you'd ever wanted, just about. Before you knew it you could not just eat whatever there was. Your body has made it quite a long way or time, but now it breaks or otherwise fails to shoot par in one way or another. Now you are married again and you are not eating some of the things that you once did, and you are eating some of the things that were once not your habit. Nowadays your body is what they call old, and you are supposed to keep track of some things that go into your stomach. Protein at breakfast. Vitamin K. Potassium. You read the sides of cereal boxes. You eat dried prunes. You eat potatoes with no salt on them.

ROOMS

For love, all love of other sights controls,
And makes one little room an everywhere.
> – John Donne, "The Good-Morrow"

THE DARKROOM

The first time I got going in a darkroom I felt a thrill, and I guess it started because a dark room is a place where scary stuff can happen. But if you are boy making pictures happen in a tray of chemicals, you are just about a magician. My bud Willy and I made that darkroom under the stairs that led down to his basement, which added, I guess, to the magic. I don't know for certain that Willy was getting a whisper of magic, but I like to think that he was. In any case, if that was reality we were watching happen in the yellow light over the trays, then we were lads in the creative gloom, altering reality, summoning it to appear. A few years later I was in the air force, working in darkrooms for my country, you'd say. I took courses in photography, learned complicated cameras to use on the ground and up in the sky. I performed optical and mathematical and chemical jobs, not legerdemain, providing information, pictures, what important people liked to call intelligence. But even though I was performing action I'd seen in a pamphlet, and even though I did it every day, up in a kite or out on the apron, or in the darkest part of the photo section, I still felt a little like a magician. I could heat up the developer, rub fingers across the sky, and make clouds appear on the brightest July day in Manitoba. It could be called science, and in secrecy it could be considered magic, or at least alchemy. You couldn't do it under the bright light of reason, and of course there is no such thing as the subconscious, and maybe you don't think a photographer should be afraid of the black, but you do have to go into the dark room to make a picture with light.

THE SMALLEST ROOM

In Greenwood the smallest room stood by
itself out in the yard between the back porch and
the chicken shed. I didn't know that some people
did it indoors, and when Saturday came and it was
time for Sally and me to have our baths, our mum
boiled water and poured it along with regular
water into the big copper tub in the kitchen. Years
later I was a copper collector under electricity
poles around Oliver, and I sold the copper tub
along with all my wire to the fat guy who sold it
for more to someone else. Back in Greenwood it
could get a little snowy in the winter, and a bare
bum on the wooden seat in that little lye-smelling
room could be reluctant. What I remember
disliking more than anything else were the sleek
pages torn from the Eaton's catalog. I used them
more sparely and carefully than I perhaps should
have. And here is an embarrassing confession if
this writing is a memoir rather than a fiction. For
those two or three years in Greenwood when I was

a little boy, I thought you were supposed to leave a little brown mark in your week's underwear. Actually. This was half a decade before the dare at Ruby's outhouse, and years before I got my picture taken at Al Purdy's famed outhouse. In the summer it was not cold sitting in an outhouse behind a house in Greenwood, but there were lots of loud and muscular bluebottle flies. I sat for as short a time as possible above those angry buzzing flies. Looking back on that little room, I now wonder why for years I would not use the toilets at school even though they were indoors when we lived in Oliver, and when we lived in Oliver we had a toilet in the smallest room indoors, though there were problems concerning that one, and now what am I confessing here? Is there a subconscious after all?

CLOAKROOMS

When I lived in small town Ontario a few years back, I heard people mentioning "the mud room." The term puzzled me for a while, made me wonder whether there were a lot of potters around town. I found out it was a little room inside the back door, where winter coats hung on pegs, and boots and galoshes were scattered around the floor, waiting for kids to put them on before heading outside. I don't know whether that's the term they use in Manitoba, but it would certainly make sense. When I was a youth in the air force in Manitoba, we called it Mudatoba. On the way into the mess hall we pulled off our flight boots and left them in a long, unheated room before heading inside to hold trays and form a line. I know that we never used the word when we were attending elementary school back in Oliver, but we had a narrow room with a lot of coat hooks at the back of each classroom, where we hung up our winter parkas and left any bags we didn't have room for at our desks. This was called the cloakroom, and I think we all knew the term was a hangover from some adult's English experience, because we may have worn coats or jackets or parkas or Indian sweaters, but we never wore cloaks. Three kinds of people wore cloaks — folks in old English books, vampires, and old country grandpas. The cloakroom got all steamy after we came in from a cold snowy January day and dumped our stuff. But when March arrived the cloakroom was pretty well empty, except for the guys who pretended they wanted to neck with the girls, or the two guys who jostled and dared each other to start a fight. Then the new Art Deco school was built, and we marched over and swarmed into our new classrooms and there were no cloakrooms, not even a whiff of cloakroom scent, just rows of coat hangers across the back walls.

DRUNK TANK

I don't remember what we did about having a pee, or heaven forbid, a crap in the Vancouver Police Department drunk tank that night, or what about the time I spent in that closet the three cops locked me in after beating me up for a while? I mean earlier in the evening I had spent some time in the Hotel Georgia beer parlour. It's a longer story and one I wrote down though I never published it. I was in for impeding a police officer in the course of his duty, which meant trying to tell Badge 27, Officer Amiel that McKenzie, the guy who had touched the other hotel's metal awning slat, had skedaddled, while my friend Mike Matthews had never touched it, having less verticle jumping ability though once a high school basketball player, and it was in good shape until Officer Amiel had bent it while yanking it loose. Anyway, the cops at the admitting desk got really pissed off at me for using the word "Canadian" when they enquired of me my nationality. Boy, they taught me a lesson. Two cops held my arms while the third drove fists into my midriff, where bruises wouldn't appear, I suppose, then dragged me by my feet to a closet and left me inside. Some time later they hauled me out and took me to the "drunk trank," and locked me in. I sniffed resentment of my education. I was the only guy in there who had been acting in a play some hours earlier. It would be my second time in jail, after a night in the Portage la Prairie slammer a few years earlier. Now about a dozen of us had to find places to sleep in a big room with fewer than a dozen steel bunk beds with no bedding. Just above the top bunks some prisoners had used lighters to burn their names or initials into the ceiling. When I think back, that's what bothers me. That those guys had lighters.

KEATS'S ROOM

Since I don't remember when, or rather since thirty-eight years ago my writing room has had two big pictures on the wall, Charles Olson the subject of one, Percy Bysshe Shelley of the other. They are two big writer figures for me, and seem to have no association with one another, but consider this: it was in Shelley's early long poem *Queen Mab* that I encountered the term "human universe," which is the title of one of Olson's most famous essays. I just now re-noticed that the Olson photo, which I acquired about forty-eight years ago, has a poem on one corner, and is a publication by Samuel and Ann Charters. Olson is seen standing with the Atlantic Ocean behind him, almost the same ocean in which Shelley drowned with a book by John Keats in his pocket. The portrait of Shelley bears a line from his early "Song" (1821) "Rarely, rarely comest thou, Spirit of delight." I bought it one day in 1980, when I went to visit the room in which John Keats died.

I suppose most people visit this room when they first come to Rome. It is next to the Spanish Steps, after all. If you haven't been there, look for it at Keats Shelley Memorial House, Piazza di Spagna, 26. You should not look to see any of Keats's personal effects where he perished of the dread consumption made worse by monstrously stupid medical treatment. The Italian authorities, acting according to standard fear of plague, burned the poet's clothing and furniture, tore up the flooring, removed the windows, scraped the wallpaper away, and replaced everything. You may visit this room, but not the things this room was made of.

OUR KITCHEN

Fancy people, we figured, said "living room" or "parlour," maybe, was that right? We never called it anything but the front room. The front room used to be two rooms, the other being my bedroom, and after my brother Roger arrived, our room. Now I can't imagine how small the front room was before we made the house twice as big as it was when we moved into town, just down the hill from my dad's school. In the years before television sets arrived in the valley, we didn't use the front room much. For bridge night, card tables would be set up and ash trays set out. There was also a little dining room with windows to the street, but until my grandfather moved in with us, we didn't use the dining room, except for holiday dinners with turkey. No, we lived the majority of our non-sleeping time in the kitchen. In the morning I brought in sawdust for the furnace and kitchen stove hoppers, and my dad started the wood fire in the little kitchen stove. The most important piece of furniture in the house was the kitchen table. We ate breakfast, lunches and supper at the kitchen table. We did our homework at the kitchen table. My father marked his students' exams there, and my mother pitted cherries there. At night we played canasta there, and after the kids went to their bedrooms, my parents played cribbage on that table. At breakfast time we pulled it away from the wall, so my sister and I could march around the breakfast table as instructed by Don McNeil on the radio. When I brought Willy or other friends home, we'd gather in the kitchen. Above the sink was a window, where my mother dumped the coffee grounds out. There was a hill of coffee grounds under that window. I wrote my first poems at that kitchen table.

GREG'S STUDIO

Greg Curnoe's artist studio was a giant version of my desk — cluttered with unfinished projects or jobs, I guess, all different from one another, but connected by his brain. Greg bought an old factory of some sort — I always thought it had been a place for making and storing cheese, but that can't be right — high over the Thames River valley, well, high by Ontario standards, down into which his tail-less cat would go, and come back addled by fresh-growing catnip. The studio was huge, as big as the rest of the house, lots of windows facing north, perfect in a traditional way for artists. I saw it when he was just getting started on it, and I saw it later than he ever would, when it contained the twisted bicycle that he was killed on. On the east wall was a number of shelves holding all the tapes of the radio broadcasts in English and Spanish made during the war of the Malvinas, which the English called the Falklands. Outside is a very tall tree with a radio aerial up its side. As far as I know, there are bicycles and bicycle wheels galore all over the studio. I remember that every time I came down from Montreal I would see a little more work on Greg's painted plywood tepee covered with pictures of members of the notorious Nihilist Spasm Band, with the stand-up-bass-shaped door, inside of which was a stool with bright words stencilled all over it. For a reason never made clear to me, this work is called "Kamikaze." I think it might be fair to use certain adjectives to characterize this wondrous room with its antique unopened pop bottles, queen-size bed, I am going by memory here, giant watercolours in stands and leaning against walls, toy fire engines and racing cars, piles of boxing magazines, books full of surrealist poetry, objects in the shape of lighter-than-air ships, what would you call it?

MY STUDY

I am writing this plain book in a little triangular room from which I can hear all the sounds in our new condominium — the washing machine not two metres to my left, the dishwasher being emptied by my sweet wife, Chopin being played through four speakers in as many rooms, and little electronic beeps coming from household appliances. I began this book by writing about my father's skull cap while sitting at a desk in our bedroom in La Manzanilla, to the sounds of grackles and the surf and the occasional dog barking in Spanish. I have done my writing in a lot of rooms in a lot of provinces and states and countries and ocean-going vessels. This little triangular room contains many objects that form constants in my life. My desk is the stained mahogany table at which Warren Tallman wrote his essays, and at which impecunious young writers snacked during parties at the Tallman house. On the walls here there are the aforementioned portraits of Charles Olson and Percy Bysshe Shelley, and other pictures of my father compared with me. Photos of my paternal grandparents, my sister and of my mother are behind me right now. There is Greg Curnoe's big painting entitled *The Woolworth Rattle*, a framed picture of Louis Zukofsky's notebook, a model of the T.S. *Estevan*, one-time lighthouse tender built in Collingwood, Ontario and employed on the British Columbia coast, a folk-art statuette of Don Quixote, a poem-painting by Kenneth Patchen (not a reproduction), a movie poster of Randolph Scott's *Ride Lonesome*, an African ceremonial shield, a Hello Kitty bank, a soccer pennant for the Berliner Fussball-club Dynamo (pre-unification), a cloth portrait of Vladimir Lenin, a brass figurine of Ganesha, and a little bust of Maimonides.

LIVING DEFENSIVELY

I seem to be writing quite a lot about my childhood. Which, though rural and western and lower middle class, was a pretty okay childhood. Eventually I had a room of my own. During our pre-teen years, though, we were interested in building forts. I never had a tree house, though I was often in trees, but I spent time in a lot of forts, natural habitat if you are carrying a wooden sword. I think that all our forts were one-room structures. Jimmy Maxwell's gang had a fort made mainly of cardboard containers, in the basement of Mr and Mrs Maxwell's house. During one of our raids my buddy Willy managed to set fire to that fort. Somehow the blaze was extinguished and we were urged to hold our raids in other parts of town. Once we turned the United Church minister's garage into a fort, complete with cans full of ashes attached to laths that were tied back with twine, ready to repel the Maxwell gang or any other assailants. We built a fort in a little cave up the hill above the school, piling rocks that would stop home-made arrows fired from any willow bows. One holiday weekend we built an intricate fort at the lumber yard, but by Monday afternoon it had been turned back into a sales place. Oh, we sometimes came home with blood on our knuckles or foreheads, from defending or attacking a fort. We built a moat once, but in the hot dry Okanagan the sandy soil would suck water away as fast as we could replenish it. My favourite fort was the pit we dug in the elementary school play yard. The boys' yard was about four acres in size, and we spent all spring digging a big pit, bringing planks to lay across the hole, ripping up native sod to lay atop the planks, then bringing sage brush and couch grass and cactuses to make the fort invisible. We had crawl holes on either side, and spent a lot of time repairing collapses. Luckily, our parents and teachers knew nothing of this very cosy dirt fort.

MAKEUP

I just now thought of the what do you call it, what do *they* call it, the dressing room? I'm picturing the room where you put on your makeup or someone else does it for you, if you are an actor in a play. Back in the day, say ages thirteen to twenty-six, when I did a lot of that stuff, when I had not settled on the few things I would be doing in my life. Back then I acted in plays by Shakespeare and Oscar Wilde and e.e. cummings and Bertolt Brecht, I was in the school band, in the choir and so on, but sitting in the dressing room, I guess, after the night's performance, digging fingers into a big jar of cold cream, and taking off my makeup, wasn't there always a tiny bit that you didn't get off, so you remembered you were an actor? At college you got to hang around in the green room and impress the freshette girls if you cared to, which I did not do much of. Starting in those years you got to keep doing the green room if the poetry reading you were going to deliver or appear in was a big enough deal. In the latter case you got to hang around with the other poets, or sometimes musicians, and there would be some people you'd think were being impressed while you remained carelessly poised. Still, nothing was really as exciting as being in that well-lit room being made up. Even the professional makeup artists at CBC television, etc. aren't that exciting. Now it is just work, you know? I never did get my own dressing room with a star on the door and flowers delivered after the performance, but my hair may have been dyed and curled. I may have been taking a quick look at the lines underlined in my copy of the script.

ELIMINATION

When, I may have said, I was an elementary school lad, I never went number two in the school toilet, which was called the "lav" in our school. I don't remember whether I had much trouble with number one. But even today I can't use the kind of pissoir they have at the Vancouver Canadians baseball stadium. It's the kind that is just a trough, and if you want to use it you have to find a place to hang out among others. I always wait for a vacant booth. In all the years I may have gone number two three times in one of those booths. I have what they call a "shy bladder." Even with individual urinals, I have been known (to myself) to pretend to have gone, did a shake-off, and zipped up. Now that I am an old gent with the attendant problems, using a public toilet is close to vexatious. Even more so when I am in a foreign country that has not securely departed the nineteenth century. It's a good time to have to urinate or deliver in Germany, say, or Switzerland, then to wash up and dry off, safe comfortable prepositions. When we visit the homes of other people, for dinner, say, I'm always watchful and careful if I have to use their bathroom. Fresh dainty towels always bother me. I usually use the big bathtub towel instead — it's easier to disguise usage that way (though you don't want them to think you didn't wash up and dry off.) And just to be safe, I always sit down to go number one, especially now that I have a long record of hospital stays and operations and the like. If you don't see that, you're a lucky young person. Even at home I have to remain conscious of my surroundings and the way I leave them. I flush no matter how gentle my visit, because we now have a large Bernese mountain dog, who understandably thinks that is her drinking fountain.

WAITING ROOM

I'm often going to see, as they put it, the doctor, the dentist, the eye doctor, the cardiologist about my defibrillator, the physiotherapist, the bloodwork clinic, the dental hygienist, and so on, and I like these occasions because I get to spend some time in their waiting rooms. It's like air travel — I get some time to read the book I'm currently on without guilt regarding the other things I should be doing, such as this. So I'm the guy who doesn't mind it when I have to wait for a doctor who is running behind schedule. Besides reading, I usually tidy the place, tossing pieces of paper into the waste basket, closing the magazines and putting them into a neat pile, etc. Of course, while reading twenty pages of Euripides, for example, I check out the other people waiting in chairs. This is what baffles and disappoints me. I swear that well over half of these people are simply sitting there, staring at nothing in front of them. How can they bear to sit there without reading? If they were women sitting in a waiting room in Germany, at least they would be knitting something. I have seen people, even people right beside me, sitting and staring in an airplane. In the airport waiting room there will be some people reading. Usually they are reading crap popular novels, but isn't that better than nothing? Better than rubbing their thumbs on the little windows in their cell phones? I look up from my Greek play in the doctor's waiting room and wonder: is there a philosophical argument going on in that person's head? I try to keep baffled scorn off my visage while I wonder: is that young person forming a refutation of his class valedictorian's address during his graduation ceremony yesterday? I return to my book, but then the doctor's assistant calls my name and I leave the fifth century until bed time, probably.

CLASSROOMS

For twenty years I sat in classrooms listening, and for forty years I stood in classrooms speaking what I was thinking. Of course I have been grateful to have a life made of reading and writing books, a life of books. Once in a while in the early years my life involved trees and trucks, concrete and ladders. I would have little flashes of fear that I would spend my life outdoors, lifting objects. I suppose you can learn things outdoors, and when I was a boy I climbed hills as often as I could, but I'm so glad that someone invented classrooms. My father spent his life in classrooms, and to a boy that appeared to be quite normal. It was formal but it seemed normal. I loved all the words I found in books, a normal place to look, and now some of the younger people I explained this to are writing books, of course they are. Sometimes in classrooms I once knew, and in classrooms I will never see, there are people standing up and explaining books. I put words into people who like books and classrooms, and some that don't, so why do we put them there? In the early years our classrooms had cloakrooms in back, but books in front, and in the early days I generally liked the books better than the people that explained them to us. I'm willing to bet that no one will ever explain this book to anyone sitting there in the classroom. I just now remember a book I was reading in grade two. It was about a boy duck sitting outside his school, listening to words coming out the classroom windows. Inside, they were talking about dropping the ten and carrying the one, and the boy duck imagined the way children might do this to numbers.

FITTING ROOMS

Some rooms are rumored to be erotic. How many stories have you heard about people joining the mile-high club in a jetliner toilet? I find it hard to believe or unattractive to picture, because when I have to use those tiny spaces I find it difficult to do what you are supposed to do in there, and usually come out with damaged elbows. A bit more imaginable is the fitting room in the clothing section of a department store. This is likely due to the fact that the experience it was intended for involves disrobing at least in part. They usually seem of flimsy building material, and have those slotted doors, and who knows the sex of the last semi-naked person in there? And you can often hear people talking near you. It's either tempting to keep the door unlocked at least, or you are so nervous that you check the little lock five times. It's hard to say which is more erotic. When you have your own pants off, how soon can you or do you get the new pants on? Now that I am a senior cityboy, I'm glad to have my wife Jean with me in that room, because she holds the other pants, and she helps me stand up to look in the mirror. She is what I used to fantasize, but she doesn't do what I used to fancy. In any case, I have someone to encourage me to buy something, and I don't have to whistle an old pop song to let them know I'm in here. I've always been excited and/or nervous to see the fitting rooms that the glossier shoppes have, those with doors or curtains that don't come all the way down to the floor. I always like to check how many feet I can see in there.

THE PRINCIPAL'S OFFICE

There could be no happy outcome if you were summoned to the principal's office. Nowadays high school teachers seem to wear pullover sweaters and talk with their students as if they were on the same side. The only time you should be scared to go to the principal's office is when he or she has to tell you someone had been in a car accident or shot. We went to the principal's office to get the strap. And you never got the strap from a woman, because in those days there weren't any female principals. So you got called, and they made you sit in the outer office, where the teachers and some of the other students could walk by and give you the white eye. Despite being a teacher's son, I got the strap twice. In grade four I called big booted Fred Collins a "clumsy oaf" for knocking me down while I was trying to field a ground ball. I got the epithet from a *Terry and the Pirates* comic. It has always been my opinion that the supervising teacher that sent me off the ball diamond didn't know what the word "oaf" meant and assumed the worst. I instinctively pulled my proffered hand away while the red-faced principal took his first shot. That did not turn out well. Later in that year a large farm girl began bashing me outside the school door, so after a while I punched her in reply. Girls did not get the strap in our school, so I faced red-face again. This time I exhibited my courage in the face of injustice, and did not use a pen or pencil for the rest of that day. Many years later I paid a visit to my old high school, and felt a wave of revulsion when I passed that pebbled glass door with the name on it.

STATEROOM

When I was a young snob I drew up an informed list of things I would never have anything to do with, largely because that's what the fraternity boys and then the Rotarians would do. Go to Las Vegas and take in the shows, for example. Get a time share in a cottage on a lake, with a big barbecue on the deck. Go for a cruise on a big ship with a Scandinavian name. Well, I haven't seen Paul Anka or Celine Dion, or those other desert Canadians, and I don't know how to cook a trout outdoors, but I have been to Ketchikan and Singapore on big white vessels. We've cruised the Caribbean and Tierra del Fuego and both canals, and managed to do it all without white slacks or a twinge of guilt. Jean and I have shared a lot of travel rooms, from one-time palaces in Spain to steel grill motels at bleak intersections in U.S. corn country. But there is nothing you can quite compare to a stateroom with a balcony upon which you can read E.M.

Forster and occasionally wave at a tanned guy on the edge of the Egyptian desert. The best room with a view is a *moving* room with a view. It's also a nice place to sleep. Sure, our bedroom on the beach at La Manzanilla in Jalisco, where I wrote the early parts of this book, features a light surf that's divine to go to sleep hearing, but to hear the faraway drone of your ship's engines through your pillow while a clear moon shows itself between your open curtains where no one in the world can look in should cost a pretty penny. And it does. And in the morning you wake atop the Indian Ocean, you have a shower while standing quite straight, and you head for the elevator that takes you to the breakfast room, where another day of choosing begins.

THE CECIL PUB

An important room in the history of Vancouver poetry was the taproom of the Cecil Hotel. We didn't use the term "taproom," though. That's the kind of word businessmen or advertisers like to use. They think it sounds sophisticated or, heaven forbid, hip. We called it the Cecil pub, which was enough of an advance over "beer parlour," and we met there once a week, on pub night. Pub night did not start until about 10:15 p.m., after the university youngsters had left for home or further fun. We were mostly poets, or writers and painters and other friends who did some kind of art. In those days the word "artist" had not been changed to mean a singer of popular music. When poets or painters were visiting from Toronto, say, they knew enough to come by the Cecil on pub night. I don't know whether esthetic discussions often transpired — we were there to gossip or catch up on each other's lives. Sometimes new chapbooks got disbursed at the Cecil. It wasn't the kind of "eatery" you get nowadays. You could get pickled eggs out of the big jar on the counter. The height of Cecil *cuisine* was an item called a "cubanette." It was so awful I can't remember what it was, but it came in a plastic bag that had been overheated in some electric gizmo, so you hurt your fingers opening the bag before you burnt your tongue on whatever was inside. Once in a while there was a barroom brawl, a chief form of entertainment in Vancouver at the time, but always with outsiders. If you were a poet and also an outfielder on a Kosmic League ball team, you did a lot of insincere bragging with teammates and foes. No one ever stood up and recited a poem. You might go home with a few typed pages, but you were not Cendrars and Apollinaire. You were never a "circle" in that large room, and nobody was allowed to take photographs in a beer parlour. Whatever brew the Cecil was serving was more important than posterity.

HOTEL ROOMS

Our hotel room in Toledo had been looking out at the Cathedral door for six hundred years. Our room in the Giulietta e Romeo hotel in Verona was fifty meters from the Roman Arena, where a big Europop show filled the streets with sound and light, lucky again, we said. On Christmas Eve in Singapore our hotel room was the site of a big holiday noise, Asiapop and cascading balloons and young people in costly raiment pretending to be drunker than they were, and we had to catch a 6 a.m. flight to Beijing. Our hotel room in Chicago could be reached via an elevator with a golden door, not exactly my kind of town, but we love the effrontery. Our hotel room in Valparaiso had a window from which we could see nothing because we were on the edge of a high cliff, and outside at the bar, young people were seated while downing pisco sours and tossing their cigarette butts a hundred metres straight down. I felt like a grubby sophisticate descending the wide staircase of the Grand Hotel in Lund, dressed like a streetcar conductor, glimpsing a royal dining court. Maybe we got the same room they had given to the U.S. president at the St. Regis Hotel in Beijing, a television set in the bathroom mirror, one Christmas carol over and over in the hallways, the best Italian restaurant you ever ate at just past the bowling alley. At the famous beat Swiss American Hotel in North Beach, back in those days, I felt very hip but someone had broken the lock to my room, and I had to do with a hook and eye. The other famous poet hotel was the Chelsea in Manhattan. My door was broken in that room, too.

THE TV ROOM

I remember the first time I heard the phrase "TV room." I had never lived in a place that had a television set in it. As far as I knew, people had the television set in their front room. Back home in Oliver, that's what my parents did, put the TV where the big console radio used to be. In my experience the TV was something you saw in the diner or in a store window. So when I got comfy enough with my new girlfriend Joan to spend some of my mature student and tyro poet time at her father's house, I saw that this house, which was apparently built by a famous architect, had a little room that was meant especially for watching TV. I figured this is what well off and sophisticated people did. I liked saying those words "TV room." I was so pleased that I was living in an age during which television was added to the ways in which to receive culture. I was young and in love and enamoured of novels and plays. In the TV room I saw *For Whom the*

Bell Tolls for a second time, with Jason Robards Jr. instead of Gary Cooper, and Maria Schell instead of Ingrid Bergman, in serious arty black and white instead of Hollywood colour in which John Donne doesn't get a mention. Got to see William Shakespeare and Samuel Beckett and Fyodor Dostoyevski in that little TV room. I blessed my lucky stars that television had come along, and that I had a girlfriend with a well-off father who had a television set that I could watch great literature on.

LOCKER ROOMS

When an unmannerly candidate for U.S. president was upbraided for telling someone (on tape) that he liked exercising his power to grab women's genitals, his spokesperson said it was all right because he was only a man employing "locker room talk." Of course he was not using it in a locker room. In fact, given that he appears tall and fat and soft, he is difficult to picture in a locker room. Of course, he used to be difficult to picture in the oval office. Remember when the Kennedy clan used to play touch football on their big Massachusetts lawn despite JFK's bad back? Now try to picture Donald Trump going deep. Anyway, locker room is an ordinary but interesting designation. Football players stomp around in locker rooms before and after bashing each other. Hockey players suit up in their bisexual outfits in dressing rooms. Baseball players will be in their clubhouse. You see why I prefer baseball to those other sports? Sure, they talk about a baseball player sitting in front of a locker. But have you seen a picture of him? There's no lock on that thing. No door, even. Now look at what is hanging in the unlocker: a shirt that buttons down the front. You want to know why basketball players like to pimp their street outfits? It's because they are not allowed to wear nice shirts at work, whether in their locker rooms or on the floor. Basketball players wear undershirts called jerseys. Football players wear jerseys. Soccer players wear jerseys. Hockey players wear sweaters, and now U.S. American sportswriters call them jerseys. If you want to dress for the game in a shirt, button up in a clubhouse. Remember the doubleknit era, when baseball players wore pullover tops? Those things and the sideburns that went with them made the game look silly, especially in Pittsburgh and Cincinnati.

BIXBY'S ROOM

My buddy Willy's father was born to British parents in China early in the twentieth century. So Willy spent his early years, before Alec ran off, with a dad who played rugby and wore old army clothes and spoke with an odd British accent. But here's why I'm thinking of Alec Lyttle here. For some reason I've never discovered he referred to their guest room in Oliver as "Bixby's room." Don't bother trying to find out anything from Google. And as these things go, Willy has always referred to his spare room as "Bixby's" room. His kid brother Sandy also used the term at his house in Winnipeg. Well, why not? Jean and I always call our guest accommodation "Bixby's room," and because it has an ensuite, we also boast "Bixby's bathroom." I'll bet that Sandy's off-spring and Willy and Sandy's sisters refer to their Bixby rooms. I hope my daughter does likewise. If the name has gone, as they say, "viral," who knows how many rooms in this world, from here back to China, Bixby could call his own, if only on a temporary basis. I have never known anyone named Bixby. I have never been to Bisbee, though I have an old sort of friend who has or had a ranch nearby. For some reason, when I heard the name Bixby, I think of William Bendix, who was in half the movies I saw when I was around twenty, but if I mentioned a Bendix room, people would likely think I was referring to the laundry room. It is peculiar, isn't it, that Bixby should have a room of his own in my house or in yours? I would like to look up something about that, but I have today had a coffee accident on Warren's table in my computer room.

ROOMMATES

If you room with someone, that is a verb, and it can happen in, say, a small number of rooms in a building. You do not need to room in a room. I did once room with a young man who made the Eiffel Tower sundae out of creme biscuits at night and lay down for electroshock therapy treatments sometimes in the day. Our landlord removed the roof from our rooms so I went to room with my friend Willy at his aunt's house up the hill. As a college student I once roomed with my aunt and uncle in Victoria, and he got hot under the collar because a young woman I was in love with came to sit in my basement room. There was a lot of room for improvement in my father's brother, and I understood why my father tended to keep a lot of room between them. Years later, when my daughter was herself at college, it did not matter whether your roommates were young men or young women, even in Victoria. I roomed with two young men and a German shepherd pup in a bunkhouse and sometimes a tent when I was a tree-marker for the B.C. Forest Service. We cooked and cleaned and once we had a fistfight. The dog ate saskatoon berries off the branch. Once in the barracks at Namao I roomed with a USAF sergeant from New Jersey, who was seldom in the room because he was in the room of a woman somewhere in Edmonton, and a skinny USAF private or whatever from Tennessee, who got really angry when I got my copy of *Sports Illustrated* with a photograph of Willie Mays and his manager Leo Durocher's wife Larraine Day on the cover. I couldn't understand him. He talked like a young man from the Ozarks, and I talked like a young man whose grandfather had come from the Ozarks. Roomies.

– La Manzanilla, January 2017 –
Vancouver, June 2018